D1433579

And there goes Juantorena…

"**opening his legs and showing his class**"

First published by Carlton Boo

Carlton Books
20 Mortimer Street
London W1T 3JW

Copyright © Carlton Books 2(

Project editor: Matthew Lowir
Proofreader: Lesley Levene
Typesetting: Liaison

A CIP catalogue for this book is available from the British Library.

ISBN 978-184732-997-4

Printed and bound by CPI Group (UK) Ltd, Croydon, CR0 4YY

Other hilarious football titles from Carlton Books include:
The Big Book of Football's Funniest Quotes
Being the Gaffer! The Crazy World of the Football Manager
1001 Bizarre Football Stories

"And there goes Juantorena...

opening

his legs

and showing

his class "

The Funniest and Daftest
Sports Commentary Ever!

Edited by Adrian Brady

CARLTON

Contents

Introduction

On the face of it, the role of the commentator and pundit must seem like the easiest job in the world. But watching sport and talking about it, as you will find out in the pages of this book, is a verbal minefield.

Let me begin by saying that commentators, broadcasters and pundits do a fantastic service in relaying the key incidents and finer details of the great sporting events to the masses, however, it doesn't always go as planned and this book is a celebration of their occasional vocal mistakes and hilarious gaffes.

Inspired by Ron Pickering's classic unintentional commentary from the Montreal 1976 Olympic Games: "And there goes Juantorena down the back straight opening his legs and showing his class", this hilarious title attempts to be the most comprehensive collection of amusing commentary gaffes and mistakes ever published.

Whether it is a confused cliché, mixed metaphor, unintentional innuendo, babbled banter or a statement of the unbelievably obvious, these brilliant quotes bring an added dimension and sense of humour to the sports we love...

Athletics

Perhaps the purest of all sports as competitors bid to go "higher, faster, stronger" than ever before. The sport's commentary calamities have a beautiful innocence about them too, with such broadcasting legends as David Coleman, Ron Pickering and Jim Rosenthal setting the standard for comic gaffes.

" False start from Darsha – it was almost as though she went before the gun went. **"**
Athletics commentator Paul Dickinson seems unsure of the principle of false starts

" She's letting her legs do the running. **"**
A detached view from athlete turned commentator Brendan Foster

It's a lovely sunny day here in the studio.
Channel 4 athletics presenter Ortis Deley

" He's 31 this year. Last year he was 30. **"**
BBC commentator David Coleman has things figured

" The Italians are hoping for an Italian victory. **"**
David Coleman

" The gold, silver and bronze will be won by
one of these five. **"**
**David Coleman stumbles over his
numbers**

One of the great unknown champions because
very little is known about him.
David Coleman

" He's got to stick the boot in, to use a
technical term. **"**
Athlete Steve Ovett

" Well, Phil, tell us about your amazing
third leg. **"**
**We think television presenter Ross King
was discussing relays with champion
runner Phil Redmond**

ATHLETICS

❝ And there goes Juantorena down the back
straight, opening his legs and showing
his class. **❞**
Athletics commentator Ron Pickering

❝ He just can't believe what's not happening
to him. **❞**
**David Coleman clearly isn't seeing what is
happening either**

❝ It's your peripheral vision that goes when
you're really exhausted; it's impossible to see
anything directly in front of you. **❞**
**Blind panic for athlete and commentator
Sally Gunnell**

❝ ...and today is the night. **❞**
**It's all as plain as day (or was it night?)
for David Coleman**

Zola Budd – so small, so waif-like, you literally can't see her. But there she is.
Commentator Alan Parry

" The theme of this year's race is Robin Hood, so here to start us off are the Three Musketeers.**"**
The race announcer at the Nottingham Marathon was gets lost in literary history

" She went off so fast she literally died in the last 50m.**"**
Let's hope Sally Gunnell called an ambulance, then

" She's literally flying on a cloud! **"**
Jessica Ennis's pole vault form was reaching stratospheric heights for radio commentator Katherine Merry

Linford Christie's got a habit of pulling it out when it matters most.

David Coleman

"Rose's brain will now be telling him exactly what to do."

A no-brainer for Ron Pickering

"Marion Jones was not flying with all her engines blazing."

Metaphors were not always a strong point for athletics legend and commentator Steve Cram

"And I can confirm that that's the fastest time in the world this year for Radcliffe – and she had to do it herself."

David Coleman sees Paula is getting no help

" Marion Jones was head and feet above everyone. **"**

Athlete and commentator John Regis obviously looks up to the champion runner

" That was an impressive run by the two English runners – one running for England and the other for Wales. **"**

David Coleman might just have offended someone's national pride

" Nobody has ever won the title twice before. He [Roger Black] has already done that. **"**

Has he or hasn't he? David Coleman confuses us all

I think there is no doubt, she'll probably qualify for the final.
Surely David Coleman is sure?

" Britain's last gold medal was a bronze in 1952 in Helsinki. **"**

All that glitters is not gold for commentator Nigel Starmer-Smith

" The reason Pinto is so far ahead is because he is going so quickly. **"**

A Homer Simpson "Doh!" moment from athletics summariser Charlie Spedding

The girls are all very tired. They have had six big events between their legs already.
Sally Gunnell

" Steve Ovett, Sebastian Coe, Steve Cram – the vanguard of our cream... **"**

Ron Pickering

" The Americans sowed the seed and now they have reaped the whirlwind. **"**

Sebastian Coe

" The Republic of China – back in the Olympic Games for the first time. **"**

David Coleman

This evening is a very different evening from the morning that we had this morning.

Sometimes David Coleman is not sure of the time of day

" He's been breaking Olympic records like nine pins. **"**

TV presenter Des Lynam

" That's the fastest time ever run – but it's not
as fast as the world record. **"**
**David Coleman might want to rethink
this one**

I'm absolutely thrilled and over the world
about it.
**Athlete Tessa Sanderson needs to come
down to earth**

" Once he'd gone past the point of no return,
there was no going back. **"**
**There was no going back for a tongue-tied
BBC athletics commentator.**

" He is accelerating all the time. That last lap was
run in 64 seconds and the one before in 62. **"**
**David Coleman seems to be having trouble
with his stopwatch**

Cram nailed his colours to the mast and threw down the Great Pretender.

Ron Pickering

" Mixed fortunes favour the brave. **"**

David Coleman

This is a young man who is only 25, and you have to say, he has answered every question that has ever been asked.

David Coleman

" Mary Decker Slaney, the world's greatest front runner – I shouldn't be surprised to see her at the front. **"**

Ron Pickering

" Christie clearly has hamstring trouble,
we think. **"**
David Coleman is hamstrung for clarity

" This is a truly international field, no Britons
involved. **"**
David Coleman

" The Americans' heads are on their chins
a little bit at the moment. **"**
Things are a bit topsy-turvy for Ron Pickering

" I have the feeling that Machado is an athlete
who likes to get away from the opposition. **"**
**David Coleman reckons that athlete
Machado Manuela is a runaway success**

" She hasn't run faster than herself before. **"**
Athlete and commentator Zola Budd

" Born in America, John returned to his native Japan. **"**
Long distance runner Mike Gratton needs some geography lessons

Ingrid Kristiansen, then, has smashed the world record, running the 5,000 metres in 14:58.89. Truly amazing. Incidentally, this is a personal best for Ingrid Kristiansen.
David Coleman

" The Kenyans haven't done much in the last two games, in fact they haven't competed since 1972. **"**
Brendan Foster

" We estimate, and this isn't an estimation, that Greta Waitz is 80 seconds behind. **"**
David Coleman

" And there's no 'I love you' message because Steve Ovett has married the girl. **"**
Does David Coleman have no sense of romance?

" The Games have been decimated. If you take away the Eastern Bloc, you take away 50 percent of the medals. **"**
Ron Pickering

And there you see Sebastian Coe preparing for our first look at him.
Jim Rosenthal

" Some names to look forward to – perhaps in the future. **"**
David Coleman

The late start is due to the time.
David Coleman

" It's a battle with himself and with the ticking finger of the clock. **"**
David Coleman

" And with alphabetical irony Nigeria follows New Zealand. **"**
David Coleman

" ...and finally she tastes the sweet smell of success. **"**
Ian Edwards gets his senses mixed up

" There you can see her parents. Her father died a long time ago. **"**
Does David Coleman see ghosts?

" He's running on his nerve ends. **"**

BBC commentator Peter West.

Ouch that must hurt

" Coe has smashed the world record
– 1:44.92 has never been run easier. **"**

Ron Pickering

A very powerful set of lungs, very much
hidden by that chest of his.

Athlete Alan Pascoe

" She's not Ben Johnson, but then who is? **"**

David Coleman

" I ran like a lemon and lemons don't run. **"**

**A sour note for British 400m runner Daniel
Caines after a poor performance**

" Moses Kiptanui, the 19-year-old Kenyan who turned 20 a few weeks ago. **"**

David Coleman

And the crowd is absolutely standing in their seats.

Ron Pickering

" And the line-up for the final of the women's 400m hurdles includes three Russians, two East Germans, a Pole, a Swede and a Frenchman. **"**

Well observed by David Coleman

" He is even smaller in real life than he is on the track. **"**

David Coleman

> And the mile once again becomes the focal point where it's always been.
> **Ron Pickering**

❝We keep thinking we have reached the bottom but then we find a new bottom. But I think we have reached the last bottom possible.**❞**
Amercian sprinter Michael Johnson on the Great Britain athletics team's bum performances

❝He only needs to be last in this.**❞**
BBC commentator David Vine covering athletics

❝Ian Mackie is here to prove his back injury is behind him.**❞**
Anonymous radio commentator

" [Steve] Backley must be looking forward to the world championships, the title really could go to anyone that's there. **"**
David Coleman hedging his bets

" Is there something that sticks out that makes you an exceptional pole vaulter? **"**
Television presenter Adrian Chiles deserves some stick for this comment

He's got so much potential and most of it still to be realised?
Commentator Stuart Storey is waiting for a good performance

" When you go into an indoors championship like this, it's different to the outdoors. **"**
Athletics coach Max Jones

Boxing

Perhaps too many punches to the head is too simple an explanation for the comic bloopers from this sport, but it would certainly account for a lot! Boxers, commentators, pundits and trainers (many of them former boxers) have brought to the ring this ding-dong comic collection that really batters the senses.

BOXING

"I'm going to fade into Bolivian."
Former heayweight champion Mike Tyson

"You can sum up this sport in two words:
'You never know.'"
**Veteran boxing trainer Lou Duva sits
on the fence about boxing**

"He's a guy who gets up at 6 a.m. regardless of
what time it is."
Does Lou Deva know what time it is?

"I don't think you can compare like with like."
**Boxing promoter Frank Warren reckons it's
beyond comparison**

"To be honest it was a very physical fight."
Jim Watt

" Lennox Lewis fought the perfect fight. He just got hit on the chin. "

Lennox Lewis's trainer following his fighter's shock world title defeat

" There's going to be a real ding-dong when the bell goes. "

David Coleman

I can only see it going one way, that's my way. How it's actually going to go I can't really say.

British amateur boxer Nick Wilshire

" His face was a mask of blood. I think he must have a cut somewhere. "

British boxing legend Henry Cooper

" My mum says I used to fight my way out of the cot. But I can't remember. That was before my time. **"**
Former heavyweight champion Frank Bruno

" I'm only a prawn in the game. **"**
British boxer Brian London

" Frank Bruno's strength, in fact, is his strength. **"**
Boxing commentator Reg Gutteridge

" Born in Italy, most of his fights have been in his native New York. **"**
TV presenter Des Lynam

" I would like to retire with brains still in contact. **"**
Boxer Herol Graham

I'm concentrating so much I don't know what I'm doing myself half the time.
Former British middleweight Mark Kaylor

" I stand a 50-50 chance if not 50-60 against anyone out there. **"**
Frank Bruno needs a maths refresher course

" I've had 38 fights, lost one and was never put on my feet. **"**
Boxing's topsy-turvy for Gary Mason

" I think it was the clash of styles that made it a good fight; we both have similar styles. **"**
Perhaps a clash of heads meant Lennox Lewis wasn't thinking straight

" Mike Tyson will have to go into a room by himself and get used to seeing the outside world again. **"**
Frank Bruno's thinking is inside out maybe?

" I truly believe that the confidence I have is unbelievable. **"**
Does Prince Nazeem Hamed believe what he's saying?

" Sure there have been injuries and deaths in boxing – but none of them serious. **"**
Former champ Alan Minter plays down the dangers of boxing a mite too much

" He looks up at him through blood-smeared lips. **"**
Boxing commentator Harry Carpenter

" Marvellous oriental pace he's got,
just like a Buddhist statue. **"**
Harry Carpenter

" Do I believe in superstitions? No. If you
have superstitions, that's bad luck. **"**
**Canadian middleweight Éric Lucas
is taking no chances**

" We'll have to take it on the chin. It's a real
body blow. **"**
**Anatomy isn't really British promoter
Barry Hearn's strong point**

" So over to the ringside – Harry Commentator
is your carpenter. **"**
BBC announcer gets tongue-tied

" I never cease to amaze myself. I say this humbly. **"**
Self-effacing as ever, US boxing promoter
Don King

" I've only ever seen Errol Christie fight once before and that was the best I've ever seen him fight. **"**
Mark Kaylor

I'll fight Lloyd Honeyghan for nothing,
if the price is right.
Marlon Starling

" This boxer is doing what's expected of him, bleeding from the nose. **"**
Harry Carpenter

"I had Bernard Taylor five rounds ahead going into their fifth round."
Former boxer turned commentator
Alan Minter

"Pedroza, the crown on his head hanging by a thread..."
Harry Carpenter

"No fighter comes into the ring hoping to win – he goes in hoping to win."
Henry Cooper

"They said it would last two rounds – they were half right, it lasted four."
Harry Carpenter

"It's not one of Bruno's fastest wins... but it's one of them."
Harry Carpenter isn't too sure

"Standing there making a sitting target of himself."
British boxing manager and trainer
Terry Lawless

"The Mexicans... these tiny little men from South America..."
Harry Carpenter needs a geography lesson

"Now it comes to a simple equation: who can stand the heat."
Harry Carpenter

It has made the richest prize in sport the richest prize in sport.
Joe Bugner

BOXING

" I don't know what impressive is,
but Joe was impressive tonight. **"**
**It's not hard to impress boxer
Joe Bugner's wife Marlene –
once she's grasped what it means**

" Magri has to do well against the unknown
Mexican who comes from a famous family
of five boxing brothers. **"**
Harry Carpenter

" Venezuela? Great! That's the Italian city with
the guys in the boats, right? **"**
**US boxing promoter Murad Muhammad
is a bit geographically challenged**

" We have an all-American boy here,
even though he is a Canadian. **"**
**National boundaries don't matter for
promoter Billy Joe Fox when talking about
signing heavyweight boxer Willie de Wit**

Cricket

The relaxed pace of the sport and the even more relaxed commentators, with hours of airtime to fill, combine to create a recipe for the occasional commentary cock-up, daft aside or hilarious double entendre. Whether uttered by Brian Johnston, Geoff Boycott, Fred Trueman or Henry Blofeld, there's never any complaint from the public as such moments have passed into cricket legend.

CRICKET

We welcome World Service listeners
to the Oval, where the bowler's Holding,
the batsman's Willey.
**BBC cricket commentator Brian Johnston
couldn't get to grips with this**

" And umpire Dickie Bird is gestating wildly
as usual. "
**Cricket commentator Tony Lewis could
have done better with a pregnant silence**

" Brian Toss won the close. "
**Close but no prize for BBC cricket
commentator Henry Blofeld**

" To stay in, you've got to not get out. "
**Cricket basics simplified for the
uninitiated by former England
opener Geoff Boycott**

❝ And the rest not only is history but will remain history for many years to come. **❞**
Commentator Jack Bannister consigns a cricket match to history

And a sedentary seagull flies by.
It was obviously a slow day for Brian Johnston

❝ The lights are shining quite darkly. **❞**
Maybe Henry Blofeld still had his sunglasses on?

❝ The crowd realises there's a match on here. **❞**
Commentator Ravi Shastri realises why so many people turned up for an India v. Pakistan cricket game

" Ray Illingworth has just relieved himself at the Pavilion End. **"**
Was Brian Johnston taking the piss?

" There were no scores below single figures. **"**
Former Australian cricket captain and broadcaster Richie Benaud gets negative

" As he comes in to bowl, Freddie Titmus has got two short legs, one of them square. **"**
Brian Johnston

" That slow-motion replay doesn't show how fast the ball was travelling. **"**
Slow motion and maybe slow wits for Richie Benaud

" And Ian Greig's on eight, including two fours. **"**
England cricket legend Jim Laker

England have no McGrathish bowlers.
There are hardly any McGrathish bowlers,
except for [Glenn] McGrath.
Stuart Law

" There were congratulations and high-sixes
all round. **"**
Richie Benaud

" Yorkshire 332 all out, Hutton ill – I'm sorry,
Hutton 111. **"**
**Digits caused a problem for BBC
newsreader John Snagge**

" The Queen's Park Oval – as its name suggests,
absolutely round! **"**
**Geometry was not a strong point for
West Indian cricketer Tony Cozier**

CRICKET

" That was intentional from Gambhir. **"**
Cricket commentator Ravi Shastri
as Gautam Gambhir hits a four

His throw went absolutely nowhere
near where it was going.
Is this Richie Benaud's idea
of a near-miss?

" England have nothing to lose here,
apart from this Test match. **"**
Former England cricketer and coach
turned commentator David Lloyd

I'm glad two sides of the cherry
have been put forward.
Geoffrey Boycott

CRICKET

" I have prepared for the worst-case scenario, but it could be even worse than that. **"**
England spin bowler Monty Panesar

" Sorry, skipper, a leopard can't change its stripes. **"**
Former Australian cricketer Lennie Pascoe

" We've won one on the trot. **"**
Former England cricket captain Alec Stewart appreciates a winning run

" We have had exceptionally wet weather in Derby – everywhere in the county is in the same boat. **"**
Kenyan cricket chief Tom Sears

" Pietersen is on the charge and on the pull. **"**
Is David Lloyd putting adoring ladies on alert for the England cricketer?

We didn't have metaphors in our day.
We didn't beat around the bush.
Fred Trueman

"Unless something happens that we can't
predict, I don't think a lot will happen.**"**
Fred Trueman

The ball came back, literally cutting him
in half.
Cricket commentator Colin Croft

"On the first day, Logie decided to chance
his arm and it came off.**"**
**A h-armless comment from Trevor Bailey
on BBC Radio**

That black cloud is coming from the direction the wind is blowing. Now the wind is coming from where the black cloud is.

Perhaps it's best that former England captain Ray Illingworth is now a cricket commentator and not a weatherman

❝ In Hampshire's innings the Smith brothers scored 13 and 52 respectively. **❞**
Henry Blofeld

❝ The wicket didn't do too much, but when it did, it did too much. **❞**
Former England captain Mike Gatting

❝ Michael Vaughan has a long history in the game ahead of him. **❞**
Cricket broadcaster Mark Nicholas

" Gul has another ball in his hand and bowls to Bell, who has two. **"**
Christopher Martin-Jenkins

This really is a fairy-book start.
Cricketer Bob Willis

" It's a catch-21 situation. **"**
England batsman Kevin Pietersen

" And there's the George Headley stand, named after George Headley. **"**
South African cricket commentator Trevor Quirk

" England have a very English attack. **"**
Cricket commentator Geoffrey Boycott

" Gary never had a nickname – he was always called either Gary or The King. **"**
Cricketer Pat Pocock

" Welcome to Worcester, where you've just missed seeing Barry Richards hitting one of Basil D'Oliveira's balls clean out of the ground. **"**
Brian Johnston sympathises with Basil

" He's usually a good puller, but that time he couldn't get it up. **"**
According to Richie Benaud, someone needs Viagra

Laird has been brought in to stand in the corner of the circle.
Richie Benaud needs to square that circle somehow

" Michael Atherton must think all his
Christmases are coming home at once. **"**
**Maybe Geoff Boycott thought
Santa Claus was next in to bat?**

He's nearly 34 – in fact he's 33.
Award that maths degree to Richie Benaud

" Gavin Larsen is inexperienced in Test
cricket in that this is his first Test. **"**
**Geoff Boycott and that first Test
problem again**

Sean Pollock there, a carbon copy of his dad.
Except he's a bit taller and he's got red hair.
**Spot-the-difference competitions are not for
cricket commentator Trevor Bailey**

There's Neil Harvey standing at leg slip with his legs wide apart, waiting for a tickle. **This sort of thing is just not cricket for Brian Johnston**

" I don't think he expected it, and that's what caught him unawares. **"**
Trevor Bailey

I think if you've got a safe pair of hands, you've got a safe pair of hands.
Cricket commentator Tom Graveney

" Anyone foolish enough to predict the outcome of this match is a fool. **"**
Fred Trueman

England might now be the favourites
to draw this match.

Spin bowler Vic Marks seems in a spin himself

❝ Mike Atherton's a thinking captain:
he gives the impression of someone
with his head on all the time. **❞**

**Thinking is more than cricket commentator
Colin Croft was doing at the time**

❝ Fortunately it was a slow ball, so it wasn't
a fast one. **❞**

Same as Geoff Boycott on this occasion?

❝ Now Ramprakash is facing a fish of a rather
different feather in Mark Waugh. **❞**

**Perhaps they were flying fish for cricket
commentator Peter Baxter**

" What a magnificent shot! No, he's out. **"**
Tony Greig

" Glen McGrath bowled so badly in his first
test as though he'd never bowled in a Test
match before. **"**
Geoff Boycott puts our brains to the test

" Nigeria, very much the dark horses of this
tournament. **"**
**The BBC commentator rightly remains
anonymous after this cricket gaffe**

" Now Botham, with a chance to put everything
that's gone before behind him. **"**
Tony Cozier

" Courtney Walsh ripped the heart out of
England both metaphorically and physically. **"**
A BBC cricket commentator gets bit gory

" He seems to have had a problem with his right foot which has run with him all day. **"**
Could English cricketer Robin Jackman expect anything else with someone's foot?

" In Australia we have a word to describe their [Pakistan's] way of playing cricket: laissez-faire. **"**
An Aussie TV commentator speaks for all francophones Down Under

" With his lovely soft hands he just tossed it off. **"**
Bobby Simpson observes strange goings-on at a Durham v. Lancashire match

" They're very experienced Test players with a lot of caps under them. **"**
Former England cricket coach Duncan Fletcher found where his players were hiding their headgear

❝ This is the sort of pitch which literally castrates a bowler.**❞**
Is this Trevor Bailey's idea of a "no ball"

❝ Strangely, in slow-motion replay, the ball seemed to hang in the air for even longer.**❞**
Cricket commentator David Acfield makes it sound like a scene from *The Matrix*

❝ A unique occasion really – a repeat of Melbourne 1977.**❞**
Jim Laker

❝ England finally cruised to a 2-0 series win over Bangladesh through the batting of Alastair Cook, who hit a 12th Test century, and Kevin Pietersen.**❞**
BBC Sport reporting that, despite their victory, the England players came to blows

❝ You almost run out of expletives for
this man's fielding. **❞**
**Cricketer turned commentator Chris Broad
swears by a colleague's abilities**

It's half of one, six a dozen of the other.
**Maybe Talksport commentator Chris
Cowdrey's maths will improve**

❝ Once again our consistency has been
proved to be inconsistent. **❞**
**Cricket coach and commentator David
Graveney doesn't consistently get it wrong**

❝ It's a difficult catch to take, especially when
you're running away from the ball. **❞**
**Is a Sky Sports commentator accusing
a cricketer of cowardice?**

Pakistan can play well, but they have the ability to play badly, too.
Cricket commentator John Embury reckons it could go either way

" As the ball gets softer it loses its hardness. **"**
Geoff Boycott stating the obvious

" If we can beat South Africa on Saturday that would be a great fillip in our cap. **"**
Metaphorically speaking, former England captain Graham Gooch didn't have it quite right

" That was a good catch from Matsikenyeri, running away from himself. **"**
A Sky Sports commentator lacking direction

" He is like a guardsman; every part of him erect. **"**
Was BBC's cricket legend Henry Blofeld
talking about stiff opposition?

" Dean Hadley has left the field with a back injury;
more news on that as soon as it breaks. **"**
Fractured logic from BBC cricket correspondent
Pat Murphy

" Zimbabwe have done well, just as it looked as
though the horse had left the stable and gone
galloping down the road, they managed to put
a chain on the door. **"**
Cricket commentator Peter Baxter rides in
with some horsey metaphors

" You can't get any earlier than the second ball
of the game. **"**
Obviously the first ball doesn't count for
commentator David Lloyd

CRICKET

" And this game is coming nicely to a climax; like a well-cooked Welsh rabbit. **"**
A BBC Radio 4 commentator gives it plenty of bunny

" You've got to make split-second decisions so quickly. **"**
Geoff Boycott's mouth was a split-second ahead of his brain

" The only person who could be better than Brian Lara could be Brian Lara himself. **"**
Colin Croft obviously rates Brian Lara

" Jack Russell may be the artist but Metson showed he's a rhyming couplet of a wicketkeeper. **"**
A BBC radio cricket report that was pure poetry

It was all so easy for Walsh.
All he had to do was drop an arm
and there it was, on the ground.
Cricket commentator Tony Lewis

" He has got perfect control over the
ball right up to the minute he lets it go. **"**
Cricket correspondent Peter Walker

" I presented my trousers to the
committee; I had nothing to hide. **"**
**Hope England cricket captain Mike
Atherton kept his boxer shorts on, though?**

" They've sent Shah in at three. It's a good
move, it'll give him time to play himself in
before he explodes. **"**
Commentator Harsha Bhogle

CRICKET

" We decided to put the foot on the pedal
towards the end – and it came off. **"**
English cricketer Paul Collingwood

" Very rare to hit a double-100 in the
50-over format. **"**
**Sky Sports' Chris Roberts didn't know
Sachin Tendulkar's 200 not out against
South Africa was so rare it was the ONLY
one in the history of ODI at the time**

" People have to realise we're the only
northern hemisphere team in cricket. **"**
**Paul Collingwood needs reminding that
the West Indies, India, Pakistan, Sri Lanka
and Bangladesh are also in the northern
hemisphere**

" Yes, he's a very good cricketer –
pity he's not a better batter or bowler. **"**
Former English cricketer Tom Graveney

Football

The world's most popular sport has made a telling contribution to sports commentary calamities. Whether it is the confused cliché, the mixed metaphor or the stating of the blindingly obvious, few sports can compare. With so many comic offerings from commentators, aided and abetted by managers and players, it is often rarer for a person to talk sense than to say something daft!

" Someone in the England team will have
to grab the ball by the horns. **"**
**Doesn't TV soccer pundit and former manager
Ron Atkinson know about the handball rule?**

I've told you a million times, I don't exaggerate.
Former Arsenal striker Charlie Nicholas

" Nethercott is literally standing in
Le Tissier's pocket. **"**
**BBC pundit David Pleat sees some strange
things in an English football match**

" Sporting Lisbon in their green and white
hoops, looking like a team of zebras. **"**
**Clearly BBC sports reporter Peter Jones
hasn't been to the zoo lately**

FOOTBALL

" He's got three goals in four games
– you can't beat that. **"**
BBC football reporter Stuart Hall

Forest have now lost six matches
without winning.
David Coleman

" Goalkeepers aren't born today
until they're in their late 20s or 30s. **"**
**That's some gestation period according
to former player and manager Kevin Keegan**

In some ways, cramp is worse than
having a broken leg.
**Not sure doctors would agree with
Kevin Keegan's diagnosis**

" Gary always weighed up his options, especially when he had no choice. "
Kevin Keegan

" You can see the ball go past them, or the man, but you'll never see both man and ball go past at the same time. So if the ball goes past, the man won't, or if the man goes past, they'll take the ball. "
Ron Atkinson... and his point was?

" Fulham needed that three points because they were slowly sinking to the bottom of the table very, very quickly. "
Football pundit Mark Lawrenson is no judge of speed

" He's been one of the best centre backs/full backs for the past 12 decades. "
Liverpool's Jamie Carragher has had a very long-playing career according to fellow player Michael Owen

Brooking trying one of those impossible crosses, which on that occasion was impossible.
Brian Moore

"When Paul Scholes gets it [tackling] wrong, they come in so late that they arrive yesterday.**"**
Time travel for Ron Atkinson

"Emile Zola has scored again for Chelsea.**"**
**A BBC Radio 5 Live commentator
sees the literary side of a football match**

"If you expose the opposition's weaknesses enough, then, in the end, those weaknesses will be exposed.**"**
Football manager Sam Allardyce

This will be their 19th consecutive game without a win unless they can get an equaliser.
BBC football reporter Alan Green

" Martin O'Neill, standing, hands on hips, stroking his chin. **"**
Do BBC sports reporter Mike Ingham's eyes deceive him?

It's now 1–1, an exact reversal of the score line on Saturday.
Radio 5 Live

" The Uruguayans are losing no time in making a meal around the referee. **"**
This match was no picnic for Mike Ingham

Poland 0, England 0, though England are now looking the better value for their nil.
Nil points for the logic of BBC sports commentator Barry Davies

"Arsenal shouldn't be too concerned, because every team has a bit of a blip during the season. Last year they had one."
Football's Ray Wilkins

I would advise anyone coming to the match to come early and not to leave until the end, otherwise they might miss something.
Football pundit John Toshack

" Peru score their third, and it's 3-1 to Scotland. **"**
There's that old maths problem again for
David Coleman

If that had gone in, it would have been a goal.
David Coleman

Ian Rush is deadly 10 times out of 10,
but that wasn't one of them.
3 out of 10 on commentary for Peter Jones

" Neil Sullivan has stopped absolutely
everything have thrown at him...
Wimbledon 1, Manchester United 1. **"**
Football commentator Mike Ingham

> And there'll be more football in a moment, but first we've got the highlights of the Scottish League Cup Final.
>
> **BBC sports reporter Gary Newbon**

" Petr Cech will want a clean sheet having been unusually leaky in the past few weeks. **"**
Match of the Day **commentator gets personal about the Chelsea goalkeeper**

" This chance is unmissable and well, er, he misses it! **"**
Football pundit Alan Hansen seems miss-tified

" After that (the Simon Davies goal), you just could smell it – Hamburg got very nervous. **"**
Summariser Chris Coleman can sniff out a victory

FOOTBALL

"Van Nistelrooy, predating as usual..."
Ron Atkinson

"Julian Dicks is everywhere. It's like they've got eleven Dicks on the field."
Britain's Metro Radio commentator makes a dick of himself

"For me their biggest threat is when they get into the attacking part of the field."
Ron Atkinson gets down to the ethos of football

"If you score against the Italians you deserve a goal."
Ron Atkinson

"Football's football: if that weren't the case it wouldn't be the game that it is."
So said the BBC's Garth Crooks

FOOTBALL

" Steven Gerrard makes runs into the box better than anyone. So does Frank Lampard. **"**
Former Premier League player and commentator Jamie Redknapp

Sometimes in football you have to score goals. **Even if you resort to using your hands, according to French footballer Thierry Henry**

" Jamie Carragher has done ever so well. He's covered up a lot of loopholes. **"**
Football pundit Phil Thompson

Portuguese international singer Cristiano Ronaldo has signed a two-year extension to his contract. **The CNN online football report announces a change of career for the player**

I would love to be able to get to the stage where things are all rosy in the garden. But I am not yet looking at pastures new, although right now we have given the critics a field day.
Football manager Alex McLeish gets all horticultural

❝ One accusation you can't throw at me is that I've always done my best. **❞**
Footballer Cristiano Ronaldo can bamboozle with this feet – or his mouth.

❝ Goodnight, and don't forget to put your cocks back. **❞**
Football pundit Jimmy Hill

❝ Henchoz advanced to the halfway line and exposed himself. **❞**
Former footballer and summariser Graeme Le Saux was on to that in a flash

FOOTBALL

" Well, Real Madrid might have got the points,
but it was an unconvincing 1-0 draw. **"**
**Sky Sport's Rob Palmer makes it far
from clear**

" We lost because we didn't win. **"**
**Could the lager be responsible for Sweden
football manager Lars Lagerback getting
tongue-tied?**

" I always want to play for my country.
I'm here if they need me for the rest of
my life, and hopefully after that as well. **"**
**Brazil's Romario is in heaven about
playing for the national side**

" It's difficult to find a defect on Mourinho,
perhaps he is a little introverted but he
is marvellous. **"**
**Inter Milan president Massimo Moratti
is not too sure about coach Jose Mourinho!**

" I would not be bothered if we lost every game as long as we won the World Cup. **"**
German football star Michael Ballack clearly hadn't thought this through

West Germany's Briegel hasn't been able to get past anyone yet – that's his trademark.
BBC sports reporter John Helm

" You don't score 64 goals in 86 games without being able to score goals. **"**
BBC sports reporter Alan Green is quite right

" It's headed away by John Clark, using his head. **"**
Football commentator Derek Rae clearly wasn't using his, though

> Celtic manager Davie Hay still has a fresh pair of legs up his sleeve.
> **Football pundit John Greig should have helped Hay get dressed**

" And with just four minutes gone, the score is already 0–0. **"**
Impressive deduction from BBC sports reporter Ian Darke

" The USA are a goal down, and if they don't get a goal they'll lose. **"**
John Helm

" And Bale slides the ball inside Cech. **"**
John Motson sees a painful pass from Spurs' winger Gareth Bale

" He dribbles a lot and opposition doesn't like it – you can see it all over their faces. **"**
Ron Atkinson

" I predicted in August that Celtic would reach the final. On the eve of that final I stand by that prediction. **"**
The BBC's Archie MacPherson knows a sure bet

" At half-time Ardiles said go out there and throw the kitchen sink at them. Spurs are doing that, literally. **"**
Doesn't former footballer Alan Mullery know that sink throwing is a red-card offence?

" McCarthy shakes his head in agreement with the referee. **"**
Body language is not Martin Tyler's strongpoint

"It was the game that put the Everton ship back on the road.**"**
BBC sports reporter Alan Green

"The ageless Dennis Wise, now in his 30s.**"**
Martin Tyler

We haven't had the rub of the dice.
Bobby Robson

"Lukic saved with his foot, which is all part of the goalkeeper's arm.**"**
Barry Davies needs a crash course in anatomy

"I'd love to be a mole on the wall in the Liverpool dressing room at half-time.**"**
Kevin Keegan

Footballers are no different from human beings.
Former England manager Graham Taylor

" I couldn't settle in Italy – it was like living in a foreign country. **"**
Liverpool legend Ian Rush on his spell at Juventus

" We keep kicking ourselves in the foot. **"**
Ray Wilkins

Burnley have the potential to be a sleeping giant.
Former England winger Chris Waddle

FOOTBALL

" I want to win the Nobel Peace Prize – and
I'm going to fight as hard as I can to make
it happen. **"**
Brazil football star Ronaldo

" Even when you're dead you shouldn't lie down
and let yourself be buried. **"**
Football manager Gordon Lee

" It's the end-of-season curtain-raiser. **"**
Former Aston Villa striker Peter Withe

" I'd like to have seen Tony Morley left
on as a down-and-out winger. **"**
**Blackpool legend and football
commentator Jimmy Armfield**

" …and their manager, Terry Neil, isn't here
today, which suggests he is elsewhere. **"**
Football commentator Brian Moore

" I'm not going to make it a target but it is something to aim for. **"**
Ex-Manchester United star Steve Coppell

The Spaniards have been reduced to aiming aimless balls into the box.
Ron Atkinson

" A few question marks are being asked of the Honduran defence. **"**
Alan Green

I think if they hadn't scored, we might have got a better result.
Former Leeds United manager Howard Wilkinson

"The last player to score a hat-trick in a cup final was Stan Mortenson. He even had a final named after him – the Matthews final.**"**
Football history is not a strong point for former manager Lawrie McMenemy

"He's got his hands on his knees and holds his head in despair.**"**
Peter Jones

"If you stand still there is only one way to go, and that's backwards.**"**
England goalkeeping legend Peter Shilton

"I had a lump in my mouth as the ball went in.**"**
Former England manager Terry Venables

"Wenger is still sweating on Sol Campbell's hamstring.**"**
Is Arsenal's website giving away medical secrets?

" Some of these players never dreamed they'd
be playing in a cup final at Wembley – but
here they are today, fulfilling those dreams. **"**
Lawrie McMenemy

" And Ritchie has now scored 11 goals, exactly
double the number he scored last season. **"**
BBC sports reporter Alan Parry

" So different from the scenes in 1872, at the FA
Cup that none of us can remember. **"**
BBC football commentator John Motson

" They can beat anybody on the day, but they
can also lose against anybody on the day. **"**
Former Liverpool football star Emlyn Hughes

" Real possession football this. And Zico's lost it. **"**
John Helm

FOOTBALL

❝ It's a game of two teams. **❞**
BBC football reporter Peter Brackley

Well, we got nine and you can't score
more than that.
Former England football manager
Bobby Robson

❝ Queen's Park against Forfar – you can't get
more romantic than that. **❞**
Archie McPherson

With the last kick of the game,
Bobby McDonald scored with a header.
Alan Parry

I am a firm believer that if you score one goal the other team have to score two to win.
Howard Wilkinson

"Football's a game of skill; we kicked them a bit and they kicked us a bit."
Former England football hard man Graham Roberts

Kicked wide of the goal with such precision.
Des Lynam

"If you're 0–0 down, there's no one better to get you back on terms than Michael Owen."
Former player and match summariser Andy Townsend

There are a whole lot of teams in the bottom six this season.
Graeme Le Saux

" There's a one-man Liverpool wall, hurriedly put together.**"**
You can count on football commentator John Murray

A run of 24 games without defeat must be a millstone on your shoulders.
Reverse thinking here from the BBC's Tony Gubba

" I'd like to think it's a case of crossing the i's and dotting the t's.**"**
Former manager Dave Bassett

FOOTBALL

"I never predict anything and I never will do.**"**
Footballer Paul Gascoigne is predictable

"I want more from David Beckham.
I want him to improve on perfection.**"**
Kevin Keegan was quite demanding as
England football manager

"For those of you watching in black and white,
Spurs are playing in yellow.**"**
John Motson

"Marseille needed to score first, and that never
looked likely once Liverpool had taken the lead.**"**
David Pleat

"They're the second-best team in the world
and there's no higher praise than that.**"**
Kevin Keegan

" You can't do better than go away from home and get a draw. **"**
Kevin Keegan reckons without the possibility of a win

Well, let's say there's no place like Wembley for the winners and there certainly isn't for the runners-up.
BBC commentator

" I saw him kick the bucket over there which suggests he's not going to be able to continue. **"**
Football pundit Trevor Brooking

" Hamburg are the European champions! **"**
ITV football commentator Brian Moore immediately after the final whistle of the 1980 European Cup final which Nottingham Forest had won 1–0

I'm not going to pick out anyone in particular, but Jay Jay Okocha should not be captain of a football club.

Former footballer Rodney Marsh

I never comment on referees and I'm not going to break the habit of a lifetime for that prat.

Ron Atkinson lets fly at officialdom

He's shown a lack of inconsistency.

Former Premier League football manager Chris Coleman

Interviewer: "Teko, what's your favourite food?"
Teko: "It's hard, but I'm going to have to say breakfast."

Orlando Pirates midfielder Teko Modise

" If ever a goal ever needed a game, this is it. **"**
Former footballer Tony Gale

Fire and broomstick.
Football pundit David O'Leary

" Well, I've seen some tackles, Jonathan,
but that was the ultimatum! **"**
Alan Mullery

" Jurgen Klinsmann, who refutes to earn £25,000
a week... **"**
**Alan Mullery reckons Klinsmann is in
denial about his pay deal**

" He's not going to adhere himself to the fans. **"**
Another malapropism from Alan Mullery

" It doesn't endow me, to be honest. **"**
Alan Mullery

I can't understand the notoriety of people.
Alan Mullery

" Will he be doing any commentaries
for us during the World Cup? **"**
" Well not unless he's going to be doing them
from the grave, Alan. **"**
Grave problem for football pundit Alan Brazil

" Our talking point this morning is George Best,
his liver transplant and the booze culture in
football. Don't forget, the best caller wins a
crate of John Smith's. **"**
Alan Brazil

“The man [Alex Ferguson] is United through and through – cut him and he bleeds red.**”**
So presumably would Alan Brazil, too

Our central defenders, Doherty and Anthony Gardner, were fantastic and I told them that when they go to bed tonight they should think of each other.
David Pleat

“I've told the players we need to win so that I can have the cash to buy some new ones.**”**
Football manager Chris Turner has a strange idea of player-motivation techniques

“Never go for a 50–50 ball unless you are 80–20 sure.**”**
BBC football correspondent Ian Dark

If we played like that every week
we wouldn't be so inconsistent.
**Former Manchester United player
Bryan Robson**

" It's hard to be passionate twice a week. **"**
**George Graham on Arsenal's
punishing schedule**

" And there's Ray Clemence looking
as cool as ever out in the cold. **"**
Jimmy Hill

That's football, Mike. Northern Ireland
have had several chances and haven't
scored but England had no chances and
scored twice.
Trevor Brooking

The Arsenal defence is skating close to the wind.

Obviously a cold wind for football pundit Jack Charlton

"And sitting on the Watford bench is Ernie Whalley's brother Tom. Both Welshman."
Brian Moore

"They've flown in from all over the world, so have the rest of the world team."
Brian Moore

Brian Butler: "Did you ever have any doubts about yourself when you left Tottenham?
Peter Shreeve: "I don't think so."

"That's Robson – a total convicted player."
Jimmy Armfield

"Peter Reid is hobbling, and I've got a feeling that will slow him down."
John Motson

"If we get promotion, let's sit down and see where we stand."
Football manager Roy McFarland

"You've got to miss them to score sometimes."
Football manager Dave Bassett

"Celtic were at one time nine points ahead, but somewhere along the road, their ship went off the rails."
Football reporter Richard Park seems all at sea

This is the first time Denmark has ever reached the World Cup Finals, so this is the most significant moment in Danish history. **Would the people of Denmark agree with John Helm?**

"The World Cup – truly an international event.**"**
John Motson

"Nearly all the Brazilian supporters are wearing yellow shirts – it's a fabulous kaleidoscope of colour!**"**
Colour is not John Motson's strongpoint

"I don't know why Glenn Murray took the penalty. I suppose because he is our penalty taker.**"**
Brighton Albion manager Gus Poyet

FOOTBALL

" Paul Gascoigne has recently become a father and been booked for over-celebrating. **"**
John Motson

" That's an old Ipswich move – O'Callaghan crossing for Mariner to drive over the bar. **"**
John Motson

" Brazil – they're so good it's like they are running around the pitch playing with themselves. **"**
John Motson

" What will you do when you leave football, Jack – will you stay in football? **"**
Stuart Hall

" Unfortunately, we keep kicking ourselves in the foot. **"**
It's painful for footballer Ray Wilkins

❝ I would not say he [David Ginola] is the best left winger in the Premiership, but there are none better. **❞**

Ron Atkinson

An inch or two either side of the post and that would have been a goal.

Dave Bassett speaking on Sky Sports

❝ Both sides have scored a couple of goals, and both sides have conceded a couple of goals. **❞**

Peter Withe, speaking on Radio 5 Live

The most vulnerable area for goalies is between their legs...

Andy Gray commentating Sky Sports

The lad got over excited when he saw the whites of the goalpost's eyes.
Steve Coppell, BBC Radio 5 Live

"If you can't stand the heat in the dressing room, get out of the kitchen.**"**
What's cooking for Terry Venables?

...but Arsenal are quick to credit Bergkamp with laying on 75 per cent of their nine goals.
Tony Gubba, BBC *Match of the Day*

"Gary always weighed up his options, especially when he had no choice.**"**
Kevin Keegan, Radio 5 Live

"We threw our dice into the ring
and turned up trumps.**"**
**Pundit Bruce Rioch reckons
football's a gamble**

...and the news from Guadalajara
where the temperature is 96 degrees,
is that Falcao is warming up.
Brian Moore

" If history is going to repeat itself I should
think we can expect the same thing again.**"**
Terry Venables

I'm not a believer in luck...
but I do believe you need it.
Former England footballer Alan Ball

"I think that was a moment of cool panic there.**"**
Ron Atkinson

Beckenbauer really has gambled all his eggs.
Ron Atkinson

"I spent four indifferent years at Goodison Park,
but they were great years.**"**
Former goalkeeper Martin Hodge

"Souness gave Fleck a second chance and he
grabbed it with both feet.**"**
Journalist James Sanderson

"They have missed so many chances they
must be wringing their heads in shame.**"**
Former England manager Ron Greenwood

FOOTBALL

" Dumbarton player Steve McCahill has limped off with a badly cut forehead. **"**
Scottish radio journalist Tom Ferrie

" A contract on a piece of paper, saying you want to leave, is like a piece of paper saying you want to leave. **"**
Former Chelsea manager John Hollins

" And I honestly believe we can go all the way to Wembley – unless somebody knocks us out. **"**
Dave Bassett

" In terms of the Richter Scale this defeat was a force eight gale. **"**
Former West Ham United manager John Lyall

" In comparison, there's no comparison. **"**
Ron Greenwood

" I would also think that the action replay showed it to be worse than it actually was. **"**
Ron Atkinson

" Mirandinha will have more shots this afternoon than both sides put together. **"**
Newcastle United legend Malcolm Macdonald

" Newcastle, of course, unbeaten in their last five wins. **"**
Brian Moore

" Certain people are for me and certain people are pro me. **"**
Terry Venables

" What I said to them at half-time would be unprintable on the radio. **"**
Former Tottenham manager Gerry Francis

"John Harkes going to Sheffield, Wednesday."
New York Post

"If there weren't such a thing as football, we'd all be frustrated footballers."
Former Everton captain Mick Lyons

He's one of those footballers whose brains are in his head
Former Rangers star Derek Johnstone

"The crowd think that Todd handled the ball. They must have seen something that nobody else did."
Barry Davies

"I can see the carrot at the end of the tunnel."
England legend Stuart Pearce

" They compare Steve McManaman
to Steve Heighway and he's nothing
like him, but I can see why
– it's because he's a bit different. "
Kevin Keegan

Glenn Hoddle hasn't been the Hoddle
we know. Neither has Bryan Robson.
Ron Greenwood

" There's no way Ryan Giggs is another
George Best. He's another Ryan Giggs. "
Scottish legend Denis Law

I don't think there is anybody bigger
or smaller than Maradona.
Kevin Keegan

Jimmy Hill: "Don't sit on the fence, Terry, what chance do you think Germany has got of getting through?"
Terry Venables: "I think it's 50-50."

❝ They didn't change positions, they just moved the players around. **❞**
Terry Venables

❝ What disappointed me was that we didn't play with any passion. I'm not disappointed, you know, I'm just disappointed. **❞**
Kevin Keegan

❝ They had to get the brassieres to thaw it out. **❞**
Ken Jones discussing a frozen pitch

FOOTBALL

" If Glenn Hoddle said one word to his team at half-time, it was concentration and focus. **"**
Ron Atkinson

" He's caused the Chelsea defence no amount of problems. **"**
Jimmy Armfield

" 80 per cent of teams who score first in matches go on to win them. But they may draw some – or occasionally lose. **"**
David Pleat

" I'd like to play for an Italian club, like Barcelona. **"**
Former Aston Villa midfielder Mark Draper needs to grab an atlas

" The referee looks at his whistle. **"**
Football commentator Dave Woods

" Well, Harry, fifth place last year,
how can you better that?**"**
Fergus Sweeney

" Macclesfield have come out in the second
half with all guns steaming.**"**
**Hot air in the commentary box
from Brian Seymour-Smith**

Commentator 1: "Looks like he's pulled his
groin and has to come off."
Commentator 2: "Yeah, he must have done
it during the one or two touches he's had in
this game…"
**Two BBC commentators debating how
Liverpool's Maxi Rodriguez got his injury**

" It's nice for us to have a fresh face
in the camp to bounce things off.**"**
Football manager Lawrie Sanchez

Golf

The world's most popular sport
has made a telling contribution
to sports commentary calamities.
Whether it is the confused cliché,
the mixed metaphor or the stating
of the blindingly obvious, few sports
can compare. With so many comic
offerings from commentators,
aided and abetted by managers
and players, it is often rarer for a
person to talk sense than to say
something daft!

" He [Ernie Els] has just got engaged which is perhaps why he produced a 69 today. **"**
Is BBC golf correspondent Tony Adamson getting a bit personal?

As the cock crows, it's only about 200 yards.
Golf commentator Peter Alliss

" A very small crowd here today. I can count the people on one hand. Can't be more than 30. **"**
Perhaps Michael Abrahamson has big hands?

" One of the reasons Arnie Palmer is playing so well is that, before each final round, his wife takes out his balls and kisses them. Oh, my God, what have I just said? **"**
An unnamed US Open TV commentator will never live this one down

What do I think of Tiger Woods?
I don't know. I never played there.
Golfer Sandy Lyle

" And now to hole eight, which is in fact
the eighth hole. **"**
Peter Alliss

" That was a beautiful shot.
Inch perfect – but an inch wide. **"**
**A BBC golf commentator just wasn't
measuring up on the day**

Some weeks Nick likes to use Fanny;
other weeks he prefers to do it by himself.
**Ken Brown talking about golfer
Nick Faldo's caddy Fanny Sunesson –
from a sporting point of view, of course**

" Pinero has missed the putt. I wonder
what he's thinking in Spanish. **"**
**BBC commentator Renton Laidlaw wonders
what "Oh, bugger" is in Spanish**

" He certainly didn't appear as cool as he looked. **"**
Renton Laidlaw

" There he stands with his legs akimbo. **"**
**Surely golf pundit Peter Alliss is pulling
someone's leg?**

" Sandy Lyle talking to Tony Adamson,
a lifetime ambition fulfilled. **"**
BBC commentator Ian Robertson

" I think Steve is the nicest guy in the world, too,
so it couldn't happen to a nicer guy. **"**
**Luke Donald is convinced about how nice
Steve Stricker is**

Peter Alliss: "What do you think of the climax of this tournament?"
Peter Thomson: "I'm speechless."
Alliss: "That says it all."
The BBC golf commentary team, men of few words

"This is the 12th, the green is like a plateau with the top shaved off."
Renton Laidlaw goes a little flat

"Notices are appearing at courses telling golfers not to lick their balls on the green."
One commentator at the 1989 British Masters golf tournament has got the double entendre licked

"I made the last putt. It just didn't go in."
Golfer Tom Kite on the difference between victory and defeat

Ballesteros felt much better today after a 69.
Is British golf commentator Renton Laidlaw being naughty?

"Azinger is wearing an all-black outfit: black jumper, blue trousers, white shoes and a pink tea-cosy hat."
Renton Laidlaw

I owe a lot to my parents, especially my mother and father.
Golf legend Greg Norman seems to have a lot of parents

"If you'd offered me a 69 at the start this morning I'd have been all over you."
Golfer Sam Torrance seems a little excitable

" Yes, Jean van de Velde is a clown,
another Frère Jacques Cousteau. **"**
Oh, brother, is Tony Adamson mixed up!

The par here at Sunningdale is 70
and anything less than that will mean
a score in the 60s.
**TV sports presenter Steve Ryder is
good at maths – and stating the obvious**

" I can't see, unless the weather changes,
the conditions changing dramatically. **"**
Peter Alliss

" Birdies wherever you look. They're coming
down like hailstones. **"**
**Former professional golfer
Ken Brown**

That's not a million miles away.
Peter Alliss

" Difficult couple of holes here – 15, 16 and 17. **"**
Former golfer Howard Clark

" And on the eve of the Bob Hope Classic
an interview with the man himself –
Gerald Ford. **"**
**Mistaken identity by golf presenter
Jim Rosenthal**

" You couldn't find two more different
personalities than these two men,
Tom Watson and Brian Barnes.
One the complete golf professional
and the other the complete
professional golfer. **"**
Peter Alliss

It's for all the gold in the world.
Peter Alliss reckons there's a fortune in golf

❝ Was I intimated by Tiger Woods? A little bit.
He's got an aroma about him. **❞**
Ben Curtis can sniff out a winner

❝ The par here at Sunningdale is 70
and anything under that will be a
score in the 60s. **❞**
**Commentator Steve Rider has his
maths right**

❝ He used to be fairly indecisive,
but now he's not so certain. **❞**
Peter Alliss

Horse Racing

Confusion in the heat of the moment as a race reaches its climax or uncertainty about whether they are referring to the horse or the rider, these are the obstacles faced by race commentators and pundits. Throw in such words as "hard", "soft" and "ride" and you can see why some have the occasional verbal fall.

She ran through the field like
water through a duck.
**What sport was former jockey and TV
presenter John Francombe watching?**

" Well, you gave the horse a wonderful ride
– everybody saw that. **"**
Television presenter Des Lynam

" Princess Anne's horse is literally eating up
the ground. **"**
**A new diet for horse-racing correspondent
Peter Bromley**

" This is really a lovely horse.
I once rode her mother. **"**
**Is horse-racing commentator
Ted Walsh giving away a
well-guarded secret?**

" ...and there's the unmistakable figure of Joe Mercer... or is it Lester Piggott?**"**
Maybe horse-racing correspondent Brough Scott needed glasses?

Tony has a quick look between his legs and likes what he sees.
***Winning Post*'s Stewart Machin speaks for all men**

" The racecourse is as level as a billiard ball. **"**
A verbal balls-up here from Channel 4 horse-racing man John Francombe

" My word! Look at that magnificent erection. **"**
You would never have guessed that Brough Scott was talking about the new stand at Doncaster racecourse

"They usually have four or five dreams a night about coming from different positions.**"**
Former champion rider Willie Carson
telling the BBC's Claire Balding
how jockeys prepare for a big race

A jockey without a whip is like a carpenter without a spanner.
Frankie Dettori obviously wasn't a carpenter before he became a top jockey

"He was going all right until he fell.**"**
Jockey John Cullen

"This is the first time she has had 14 hands between her legs.**"**
John Francome

> A lot of horses get distracted.
> It's just human nature.
> **Horse trainer Nick Zito**

" In this yard, all horses are treated equally, but there is one animal that knows he's a little more equal than the others. **"**
Equality comes unequally in a BBC News item about star horse Kauto Star event

" The bookies are literally waltzing out of here under cloud nine. **"**
Commentator Colm Murray at the Cheltenham Festival

" At Ascot today the heat is quite hot. **"**
BBC presenter Judith Chalmers at a flat-racing event

Motorsport

In a few of the sports already featured one or two names keep cropping up, but nothing like to the degree that Murray Walker dominates motorsport commentary faux pas. His infectious enthusiasm, confused descriptions and gift for speaking without thinking make him a standout comic commentator. Add to this his apparent ability to jinx the driver he is discussing and you have a broadcaster whose "Murrayisms" will remain in sports commentary folklore forever.

Do my eyes deceive me or is
Senna's Lotus sounding rough?
**Aural cock-up from Grand Prix
commentator Murray Walker**

" Alboreto has dropped back up to fifth place. **"**
**Murray Walker seems to have misplaced
a Formula One driver**

I can't imagine what kind of problem Senna has.
I imagine it must be some sort of grip problem.
Murray Walker

" The drivers have one foot on the brake,
one on the clutch and one on the throttle. **"**
**Speed Channel's Bob Varsha pedalling
some nonsense**

MOTORSPORT

" It's basically the same, just darker. **"**
No change, then, for stock-car racer
Alan Kulwicki on switching Saturday
night racing to Sunday afternoons

" I kind of like to have someone looking up my arse. **"**
Former IndyCar and Formula One driver
Mario Andretti

" Schumacher virtually pedalling his
Benetton back with his fists. **"**
According to Murray Walker, the German
F1 driver was adding extra punch

" There are enough Ferraris to eat
a plate of spaghetti. **"**
Former Grand Prix champion
Jackie Stewart

❝ Ericsson's record is second to none in the RAC Rally; he's been second three times. **❞**
A Mitsubishi Motors spokesman doesn't quite get the point

❝ He is shedding buckets of adrenalin in that car. **❞**
Murray Walker makes it sound messy

Murray Walker: "So Bernie [Ecclestone], in the 17 years since you bought McLaren, which of your many achievements do you think was the most memorable?"
Bernie Ecclestone: "Well, I don't remember buying McLaren."
One team was obviously much the same as another for Walker, because Ecclestone owned Brabham

" A mediocre season for Nelson Piquet
as he is now known and always has been. "
Murray Walker

" Alain Prost is in a commanding second position. "
Murray Walker

" Speaking from memory, I don't know how
many points Nelson Piquet has. "
Murray Walker

" Thackwell really can metaphorically coast
home now. "
Murray Walker

" What does it feel like being rammed up the
backside by Barrichello? "
**Commentator James Allen gets personal
when interviewing F1 driver Ralf Schumacher**

" And now Jacques Laffite is as close
to Surer as Surer is to Laffite. **"**
Murray Walker

" Nigel Mansell is the last person in the
race apart from the five in front of him. **"**
Murray Walker

Murray Walker: "What's that? There's a body
on the track!!!
Co-presenter: "Um, I think that that is a piece
of bodywork, from someone's car."
Things are not always as they appear

" Jenson (Button) is literally putting his balls
on the line going up against Lewis. **"**
Formula One summariser David Coulthard

I don't want to tempt fate but Damon Hill is now only half a lap from his first Grand Prix win and...and... he's slowing down, Damon Hill is slowing down... he's... he's stopped.
Did Murray Walker put the mockers on Hill?

"Cruel luck for Alesi, second on the grid. That's the first time he had started from the front row in a Grand Prix, having done so in Canada earlier this year."
Murray Walker's knowledge is second to none

And there's the man in the green flag!
Murray Walker

> **Murray Walker:** "And look at the flames coming from the back of Berger's McLaren.
> **Co-presenter:** "Actually, Murray, they're not flames, it's the safety light."

" ... and there's no damage to the car... except to the car itself. **"**
Murray Walker contradicts himself

" This is an interesting circuit because it has inclines, and not just up, but down as well. **"**
The ups and downs of being Murray Walker

" Only a few more laps to go and then the action will begin, unless this is the action, which it is. **"**
Murray Walker

Tombay's hopes, which were nil before, are absolutely zero now.
Murray Walker gets negative

"You can't see a digital clock because there isn't one.**"**
Murray Walker

"The Italian GP at Monaco...**"**
Geography's not Murray Walker's strong point sometimes

"...the enthusiastic enthusiasts...**"**
Grand Prix tautology from Murray Walker

"As you can see, visually, with your eyes...**"**
Can Grand Prix viewers see what Murray Walker is getting at?

" Andrea de Cesaris... the man who has won more Grands Prix than anyone else without actually winning one of them. **"**
A confused Murray Walker

" And we have had five races so far this year, Brazil, Argentina, Imola, Schumacher and Monaco! **"**
Murray Walker

" And Damon Hill is coming into the pit lane... yes, it's Damon Hill coming into the Williams pit, and Damon Hill in the pit... no, it's Michael Schumacher! **"**
A case of mistaken identity for Murray Walker

" Mansell is slowing it down, taking it easy. Oh no, he isn't! It's a lap record. **"**
Murray Walker

" Into lap 53, the penultimate last lap but one. **"**
Things don't add up for Murray Walker

There are a lot of ifs in Formula One,
in fact IF is Formula One backwards!
Murray Walker

" And that just shows you how important
the car is in Formula One racing. **"**
Murray Walker is dead right about that

" A battle is developing between them.
I say developing, because it's not yet on. **"**
Murray Walker gets his crystal ball out

" A sad ending, albeit a happy one. **"**
Murray Walker

" And Edson Arantes di Nascimento,
commonly known to us as Pelé,
hands the award to Damon Hill,
commonly known to us as Damon Hill. **"**
Murray Walker

" And Michael Schumacher is actually in
a very good position. He is in last place. **"**
**Don't think Schumacher would agree
with Murray Walker**

" And now, excuse me while I interrupt
myself. **"**
Murray Walker

" Are they on a one-stopper? Are they on a two?
And when I say they, who do I mean?
Well, I don't know. It could be anybody. **"**
**One of those confused days for
Murray Walker**

" Either the car is stationary, or it's on the move. **"**
Murray Walker

" Even in five years' time, he will still be
four years younger than Damon Hill. **"**
Murray Walker has got it figured...

" Fantastic! There are four different
cars filling the first four places. **"**
Murray Walker states the obvious

" He can't decide whether to leave
his visor half open or half closed. **"**
Murray Walker got it half right

" I don't know what happened, but there was a
major malmisorganisation problem there. **"**
**Murray Walker has a "malmisorganisation
problem" with his mouth**

"I should imagine that the conditions in
the cockpit are totally unimaginable.**"**
Murray Walker uses his imagination

I've no idea what Eddie Irvine's orders are, but
he's following them superlatively well.
Murray Walker

"If the gloves weren't off before,
and they were, they sure are now!**"**
Murray Walker

Colin had a hard on in practice earlier,
and I bet he wished he had a hard on now.
**No, really, World Superbike racing
commentator Jack Burnicle was talking
about Colin Edwards's tyre choice**

Ralf Schumacher speaking in German for our English listeners.
English listeners would have been as mystified as BBC Radio's Eleanor Oldroyd obviously was

" It looks as though this year there will be 17 Grands Prix for the World Championship, compared with the traditional 17. **"**
Murray Walker should check his notes

" Now he must not go the wrong way round the circuit, and unless he can spin himself stationary through 360 degrees I fail to see how he can avoid doing so. **"**
Murray Walker gets it wrong by degrees

" In 12th and 13th, the two Jaguars of Eddie Irvine. **"**
Murray Walker is seeing double

Prost can see Mansell in his earphones.
**Murray Walker reckons Alain
had got eyes each side of his head**

❝ So this being Michael Schumacher's
10th race in his 151st year in F1. ❞
**Murray Walker makes Schumacher
a real veteran driver**

The boot's on the other Schumacher now!
Murray Walker

❝ The lead car is unique, except for
the one behind it, which is identical. ❞
Murray Walker

" There are seven winners of the Monaco
Grand Prix on the starting line today,
and four of them are Michael Schumacher. "
**Oh no! Murray Walker's seeing double
double now**

" Veteran BBC commentator Murray Walker
said it was the blackest day for Grand Prix racing
since he had started covering the sport. "
**This BBC Teletext news piece should have
been checked before transmission, it seems**

" Mark Blundell stops with his front
wheels stationary. "
**Murray Walker can sense a bit of
inertia here**

" Since I have been here at McLaren, we have
never really had an amazing rear end. "
**Lewis Hamilton speaking about his car
– not the cheerleaders in the pit area**

> There's nothing wrong with
> the car except that it's on fire.
> **Murray Walker fans the flames
> of uncertainty**

" This will be Williams's first win
since the last time a Williams won. **"**
Murray Walker

> Well, now we have exactly the same
> situation as at the beginning of the race,
> only exactly the opposite.
> **Murray Walker turns things upside down**

" Red Bull will be really worried about the blue
smoke coming from the back of Mark Webber. **"**
Martin Brundle

" The first four cars are both on the same tyres. **"**
Murray Walker must have been a bit tyred
himself to broadcast this

He's only 19. That's the same age
Eddie Irvine was when he was 19.
The BBC Radio 5 Live commentator
wasn't wrong, either

" Even as I speak, in four hours' time
the Kyalami Grand Prix will roar away. **"**
Commentator Tony Lewis

The lead is now 6.9 seconds.
In fact it's just under 7 seconds.
Murray Walker

" I wonder if Watson is in the
relaxed state of mind he's in. **"**
Murray Walker

" Your luck goes up and down
like swings and roundabouts. **"**
Former Grand Prix champion
James Hunt

" I make no apologies for their absence.
I'm sorry they're not here. **"**
Murray Walker is sorry for himself

" If McLaren hadn't gone for Jenson (Button),
they'd have gone for someone else. **"**
There's no fooling Kimi Raikkonen's
manager

This is lap 54. After that, it's 55, 56, 57, 58 and 59.

You can count on Murray Walker's figures

"The gap between the two cars is 0.9 of a second, which is less than one second."

Murray Walker's got it figured

The faster he goes, the quicker he'll get to the pits. The slower he goes, the longer it will take.

Murray Walker on the principles of speed

"Tambay's hopes, which were nil before, are absolutely zero now."

Murray Walker

> You might not think that's cricket,
> and it's not, it's motor racing.
> **Murray Walker thinks we might
> be confused about the difference**

" The young Ralf Schumacher has been
upstaged by the teenager Jensen Button,
who is 20. **"**
Murray Walker got it a teen-y bit wrong

" He [Damon Hill] doesn't know –
but if anyone knows he would. **"**
**Don't know what Murray Walker
knows about this**

" Look up there! That's the sky! **"**
Murray Walker seems surprised

" You can cut the tension with a cricket stump. **"**
Murray Walker gets a bit heavy-handed

" If that's not a lap record, I'll eat the hat I don't normally wear. **"**
Murray Walker

That's history. I say history because it happened in the past.
Murray Walker gets nostalgic

" There's so many celebrities on this grid, I can hardly see the wood for the trees. **"**
Martin Brundle

Rugby

Cryptic commentary, daft insights, mixed-up metaphors and some unintentional innuendo form the bedrock of these rugby commentary calamities. Whether it is rugby league or rugby union, these will have the scrum rolling in the mud with laughter.

" If I've seen two more competitive players
than Armstrong and Van der Westheizen,
I've yet to see them. **"**
**An "are they or aren't they?" conundrum
for former Scotland rugby union captain
and pundit Gavin Hastings**

" This lad's a butcher – but I've never had
any of his meat. **"**
Rugby league commentator Eddie Waring

" They've got their heads in the sand.
It's a Canute job. **"**
**A mixed-up rugby union commentator
gets his metaphors in a twist**

" And the blue and white hoops of Sale will
no doubt act as a red flag to the Tigers. **"**
**Colourful commentary from the BBC's
Ian Brown**

And there's Gregor Townsend's knee,
looking very disappointed.
Gavin Hastings

" The ball is often a handicap in these conditions. **"**
Former rugby player and commentator
Nigel Starmer-Smith finds his tongue a
handicap, too

…and, in contrast, we have the New Zealand
team littered with internationals.
The BBC commentator has no surprises
for the Kiwis

" I don't know where Jonny Wilkinson is.
I do know where he is, he's not there. **"**
Former rugby player Brian Moore

❝ Nigel Starmer-Smith had seven craps for England some years ago. **❞**
Presenter and pundite Jimmy Hill

Reporter: "What of the future for Welsh rugby?"
Welsh captain Mike Watkins: "Over to the Angel for a lot of pints."

❝ Condom is back in French pack. **❞**
Was this rugby union headline in the *Independent* newspaper in French letters?

❝ Rafter again doing much of the unseen work which the crowd relishes so much. **❞**
Rugby commentator Bill McLaren

The French selectors never do anything
by halves; for the first international of the
season against Ireland they dropped half
the three-quarter line.
**Give Nigel Starmer-Smith half
a chance and he'll get it wrong**

"A lot of these guys have waited a lifetime
not to win this."
**Aussie rugby union star David Campese
had waited a lifetime not to get this
broadcast right**

We go to the four corners of the globe
to bring you the best of rugby league
– Batley, Oldham, Wigan and France.
**Geography lesson needed for
commentator Eddie Hemmings**

" We all know England are the best rugby team in the world and next weekend, when they play Scotland, we'll find out if they are the best in Britain. **"**
Lord Archer obviously rates Britain highly

" Scotland were victims of their own failure. **"**
Gavin Hastings

" We are committing our own suicide. **"**
Suicide is so personal for Scotland rugby union team coach Ian McGeechan

" Hopefully the rain will hold off for both sides. **"**
Unbiased rain – just what rugby union star Lawrence Dallaglio wanted

" They're a bit laxative. **"**
Rugby league's Robbie Paul is a bit lackadaisical with words

" Andrew Mehrtens loves it when
Daryl Gibson comes inside of him. **"**
**New Zealand rugby commentator's
vocal slip-up**

" There's no such thing as a lack of confidence.
You either have it or you don't. **"**
England rugby international Rob Andrew

" ...And Dusty Hare kicked 19 of the 17 points. **"**
**David Coleman covers rugby for a change
and struggles with the scoring system**

" Frustration was the buzzword in the squad
on Saturday. **"**
Former England coach Martin Johnson

" We have self-belief in each other. **"**
A very believable Gavin Hastings

" The ref's turned a blind ear. **"**
New Zealand rugby union commentator
Murray Mexted

And he's got the icepack on his groin there,
so possibly not the old shoulder injury.
That medical degree came in handy for
rugby commentator Ray French

" I don't like this new law, because your first
instinct when you see a man on the ground
is to go down on him. **"**
Murray Mexted

" I am not getting any younger and there
are a few other guys in the same situation. **"**
Age begins to tell on England's Nick Easter

You don't like to see hookers
going down on players like that.
**Double-entendre specialist
Murray Mexted strikes again...**

"He's looking for some meaningful
penetration into the backline."
... and again...

I just love it when Mehrtens
comes on the inside of Marshall.
Murray Mexted can't stop himself

"Everybody knows that I have
been pumping Martin Leslie for
a couple of seasons now."
Another Murray Mexted classic

Snooker

Perhaps these are a commentators' cries for help or just for their own amusement as they are forced to report on an intense game from a dark, clammy studio for hours on end. Whatever the reason, though, snooker has blessed this book with daft sporting quotes in abundance. It also seems as if some commentators have never really understood the technology of television, with bizarre advice on which colour ball to look out for if you are watching on a black and white television set!

" 99 times out of 1,000 he would have potted that ball. **"**
Snooker commentator Ted Lowe

" And [Terry] Griffiths has looked at that blue four times now – and it still hasn't moved. **"**
Ted Lowe expects Griffiths to do great things with his eyes but wouldn't a cue be easier?

" He's lucky in one sense and lucky in the other. **"**
Ted Lowe

" What Graeme Dott likes to do is win frames. **"**
Snooker's Steve Davis

" The audience are literally electrified and glued to their seats. **"**
Sticky situation for Ted Lowe

Oh, that's a brilliant shot. The odd thing
is his mum's not very keen on snooker.
Ted Lowe

" [Alex] Higgins first entered the championship
10 years ago. That was for the first time,
of course. **"**

Ted Lowe chalks up a definite first

" And it is my guess that Steve Davis will try to
score as many points as he can in this frame. **"**

**Ted Lowe has at least got the point of
snooker nailed down**

" Steve Davis has a tough consignment in front
of him. **"**

**Ted Lowe obviously thinks the player
comes with a lot of baggage**

A little pale in the face, but then his name is White.

Ted Lowe a little red-faced over this comment?

" That pot puts the game beyond reproach. **"**

Ted Lowe goes in for the blame game

All square, all the way round.

Ted Lowe squares the circle

" There is, I believe, a time limit for playing a shot. But I think it's true to say that nobody knows what the limit is. **"**

Ted Lowe needs a rule book

Jimmy White has that wonderful gift of being able to point his cue where he is looking.
Ted Lowe reckons there's no room for cross-eyed snooker players, then?

" When you start off, it's usually nil-nil. **"**
Former snooker champion Steve Davis's starter for 10

Just enough points here for Tony to pull the cat out of the fire.
Can TV snooker commentator Ray Edmonds smell burning fur somewhere?

" Suddenly Alex Higgins is 7–0 down. **"**
TV snooker commentator David Vine seemed to have lost track of time

" Tony Meo is beginning to find his potting boots. **"**
Former player and snooker commentator Rex Williams

From this position you've got to fancy either yourself or your opponent winning.
Snooker player and pundit Kirk Stevens sits on the fence

" The match has gradually and suddenly come to a climax. **"**
David Vine isn't too sure about this, though

No one came closer to winning the title last year than the runner-up.
Snooker player and commentator Dennis Taylor

SNOOKER

❝ I've always said the difference between
winning and losing in nothing at all. **❞**
Snooker legend Terry Griffiths

❝ Valour was the better part of discretion there. **❞**
**TV snooker commentator Jack Karnehm
mixes his metaphors**

❝ Sometimes the deciding frame is
always the hardest one to win. **❞**
Dennis Taylor

❝ That said, the inevitable failed to happen. **❞**
**TV snooker commentator John Pulman
was inevitably wrong about that**

❝ 10–4 and that could mean exactly what it means. **❞**
Well, David Vine knows what HE means

And now for some snooker news: Steve Davis has crashed out of the UK Billiards Championship.

Snooker player and commentator Allan Taylor gets his green baize sports in a mixed up

---

" Ray Reardon is one of the great Crucible champions. He won it five times when the championship was played away from the Crucible. **"**

David Vine misses his own point

" And that's the third time this session he's missed his waistcoat pocket with the chalk. **"**

Eagle-eyed Ted Lowe

" There are those with commentators' eyes, and then there's Willie Thorne. **"**

John Virgo

SNOOKER

" Steve is going for the pink ball – and for those of you who are watching in black and white, the pink is next to the green. **"**
Colourful commentary from Ted Lowe

" And this is, as they say, what happens next. **"**
David Vine comes over clairvoyant

" Jimmy White is known as 'The Nearly Man' of snooker, but a lot of people forget that he's got the second best record in the world championship in the 1990s. **"**
Does snooker ace Steve Davis reckon White is second to none?

" At certain times here, and even in the hotel, there's nearly a stench of death in the place. **"**
Snooker is life and death for Irish star Fergal O'Brien

SNOOKER

" For those of you watching who do not have
TV sets, live commentary is on Radio 2. **"**
Ted Lowe mystifies viewers and listeners

" Stephen Hendry jumps on Steve Davis's misses
every chance he gets. **"**
**This didn't come out quite how Eurosport
snooker commentator Mike Hallet intended**

" He won't be able to pot that red unless
he manages to hit it. **"**
**Former snooker player and commentator
John Virgo reckons Jack Doherty's game
can be hit and miss**

" There's no better feeling than getting
a century break... and getting one at the
Crucible is even better. **"**
Commentator Willie Thorne

Fred Davis, the doyen of snooker. Now 67 years of age and too old to get his leg over, prefers to use his left hand.

Commentator Ted Lowe was referring to snooker, of course

"If you get to 9-7...you start seeing alarm bells then.**"**

Commentator John Parrot

"It's all about the length and this one doesn't look hard enough to me.**"**

Is John Virgo being rude?

"This is where the precision has to be precise.**"**

Former snooker player John Spencer knows precisely

Tennis

In this chapter you will find some marvellous examples of commentators and players stating the blindingly obvious. Whether they feel they are doing the general public a service or perhaps just desperately trying to fill some airtime in a long and uneventful match, I am not sure. All I know is that the volley of queer quotes makes for hilarious reading.

And here's Zivojinovic, six feet six inches tall and 14 pounds 10 ounces.
BBC tennis commentator Dan Maskell makes light of the player

" Martina, she's got several layers of steel out there, like a cat with nine lives. **"**
Wimbledon champion and BBC tennis commentator Virginia Wade's analogies can be a bit bewildering

" The Gullikson twins here. An interesting pair, both from Wisconsin. **"**
Dan Maskell

" It's quite clear that Virginia Wade is thriving on the pressure now that the pressure on her to do well is off. **"**
BBC commentator Harry Carpenter's on-off comments

" Billie Jean King, with the look on her face that says she can't believe it... because she never believes it, and yet, somehow, I think she does. "
Unbelievable comments from BBC tennis pundit Max Robertson

I'm an American. You can't go on where you were born. If you do, then John McEnroe would be a German.
Pundit and tennis legend Martina Navratilova misplaces Mac's heritage

" As Boris Becker sits there, his eyes staring out in front of him, I wonder what he's thinking. I think he's thinking, 'I am Boris Becker.' At least I hope that's what he's thinking. "
Methinks the BBC's John Barrett wasn't thinking before he started speaking...

" You can always feel much better if someone endorses the call – even if they are wrong. **"**
Virginia Wade

Sampras's heart must have been in his hands. **I've heard of wearing your heart on your sleeve but this Sky commentator sees more**

" I wonder if the Germans have a word for *Blitzkrieg* in their language. **"**
***Achtung!* A language gaffe from South African tennis pundit Frew McMillan**

" Nobody is blaming the linesman. Of course, he did make a couple of big mistakes. Really big ones. **"**
Tennis star Marat Saffin makes his point on officialdom

" I have a feeling that, if she had been playing herself, she would have won that point. **"**
Former Australian tennis player and commentator Bob Hewitt

Getting your first serve in is a great way to avoid double faults. **"**
Former Australian tennis player John Fitzgerald serves up the obvious for tennis fans

" Martina Hingis is going through a part of her life which she has never been through before. **"**
BBC tennis commentator

" Federer is human, but for how long? **"**
BBC tennis commentator

Miss Stove seems to be going off the boil.
Tennis commentator Peter West likes a pun

" If you can't get near a radio, Henman's taken the first set. **"**
A bit of radio ga-ga from BBC Radio 1

Sampras, in white, serves with his baggy shorts.
The BBC's Ian Carter has a theory about why Pete's balls were nearly always in

" These ball boys are marvellous.
You don't even notice them.
There's a left-handed one over there.
I noticed him earlier. **"**
Max Robertson

TENNIS

" She never loses a match. If she loses a match, it's because her opponent beats her. **"**
Former tennis player and commentator Pam Shriver seemed a little confused

She comes from a tennis-playing family. Her father's a dentist.
BBC commentator

" Well, judging from his serves, Larsson will either win this match or lose it. **"**
A Eurosport commentator was definitely hedging his bets

" Tennis is one of those games like all other games. **"**
Wimbledon champion Virginia Wade doesn't think tennis is unique

Other
Sports

Unintentional sports commentary slip-ups aren't confined to the major sports. Cycling, darts, Gaelic football, swimming, weightlifting and wrestling, have all made hilarious contributions to this compendium of comic commentary.

" In cycling you can put all your money on one horse. **"**
Cycling legend Stephen Roche changes saddles.

And this is Gregoriava from Bulgaria. I saw her snatch this morning and it was amazing!
Weightlifting commentator Pat Glenn is open to interpretation

" It's obvious these Russian swimmers are determined to do well on American soil. **"**
Olympic swimming champion Anita Lonsborough

" Teddy McCarthy to John McCarthy, no relation, John McCarthy back to Teddy McCarthy, still no relation... **"**
Gaelic football commentator Michael O'Muircheartaigh

OTHER SPORTS

" Under that heart of stone beats muscles of pure flint. **"**
Darts, rather than anatomy, was commentator Sid Waddell's strongpoint

" It was the fastest-ever swim over that distance on American soil. **"**
Swimmer Greg Phillips gets down and dirty

" The swimmers are swimming their socks off. **"**
Wet socks for Olympic star Sharron Davies

" He's been burning the midnight oil at both ends. **"**
So has darts expert Sid Waddell by the sound of it

" This seesaw's going up and down like a roundabout, what a match! **"**
Sid Waddell

What a man, what a lift, what a jerk!
Jimmy McGee on weightlifting in the Olympic Games

" ...and so they have not been able to improve their 100 per cent record. **"**
BBC Sports Round-up

" Only one word for it – magic darts. **"**
Darts commentator Tony Green

" Oh dear, he's laddered his tights. **"**
ITV wrestling commentator Kent Walton

The harder it is, the more difficult.
A bit obvious from a BBC TV commentator

OTHER SPORTS

" 3–0 Finland and Russia are lucky to get nothing. "
No credit for the Russians from the BBC's ice hockey commentator

" If our swimmers want to win any more medals, they'll have to put their skates on. "
Does Dave Brenner want swimming on ice?

" These American horses know the fences like the back of their hands. "
Former show jumper Harvey Smith

" He's a very competitive competitor, that's the sort of competitor he is. "
Equestrian commentator Dorian Williams

" The conclusion is drawing to a conclusion. "
BBC presenter Ray Stubbs

United Sports of America

They claim that everything is bigger and better in America, and that can certainly be said about the amount of babbled banter spouted in the name of their sports. Whether it's American football, baseball or basketball, the Yanks prove they are a real superpower in the world of the comic sporting slip-up.

American football

Rapport? You mean like, "You run as fast as you can, and I'll throw it as far as I can?"
Jeff Kemp, 49ers football quarterback, simplifies his relationship with wide receiver Jerry Rice

I'm not allowed to comment on lousy officiating.
Jim Finks, New Orleans Saints general manager, pushes his luck with officialdom

Baseball

" When you get that nice celebration coming into the dugout and you're getting your ass hammered by guys – there's no better feeling than to have that done. **"**
Is baseball star Matt Stairs revealing too many secrets

" Rich Folkers is throwing up in the bullpen. **"**
Former baseball player and commentator
Jerry Coleman thinks he might be sick
of baseball

" When you come to a fork in the road, take it! **"**
Baseball's Yogi Berra speaks with forked tongue

" Always go to other people's funerals;
otherwise they won't go to yours. **"**
Yogi Berra wants his friends back from
the dead

" I knew the record would stand until it was broken. **"**
Yogi Berra

" Baseball is 90 per cent mental. The other half
is physical. **"**
Yogi Berra has a maths problem

Basketball

I told him, "Son, what is it with you. Is it ignorance or apathy?" He said, "Coach, I don't know and I don't care."
Utah Jazz president Frank Layden's exchange with a player

"We can't win at home. We can't win on the road. I just can't figure out where else to play.**"**
There's no middle way for Pat Williams, Orlando Magic's general manager

Son, looks to me like you're spending too much time on one subject.
Texas A&M coach Shelby Metcalf is honest with a player who academically got four Fs and one D

Left hand, right hand, it doesn't matter.
I'm amphibious.
**Former pro Charles Shackleford might
be a handy guy to swim with**

"We're going to turn this team around
360 degrees."
**Basketball player Jason Kidd is back
where he started**

Reporter: "Did you visit the Parthenon
while in Greece?"
Basketball star Shaquille O'Neill:
"I can't really remember the names of all
the clubs we went to."

My sister's expecting a baby,
and I don't know if I'm going to be
an uncle or an aunt.
**Relationships aren't a strong
point for North Carolina State
player Chuck Nevitt**

" He has the players too happy. **"**
**Boston Celtics' general manager Red
Auerbach is critical of Bill Russell's coaching**

" He treats us like men. He lets us wear earrings. **"**
**Houston University receiver Torrin Polk
is so grateful to his coach**

" Tom. **"**
**The answer given by the Houston Rockets'
Tom Nissalke when asked how he pronounced
his name**